HALLOWEEN

BY HALEY WILLIAMS

Core Library

An Imprint of Abdo Publishing
abdobooks.com

Cover image: Some Halloween costumes involve symbols such as pumpkins or bats. Orange, purple, and black are common Halloween colors.

abdobooks.com

Published by Abdo Publishing, a division of ABDO, PO Box 398166, Minneapolis, Minnesota 55439. Copyright © 2024 by Abdo Consulting Group, Inc. International copyrights reserved in all countries. No part of this book may be reproduced in any form without written permission from the publisher. Core Library™ is a trademark and logo of Abdo Publishing.

Printed in the United States of America, North Mankato, Minnesota.
102023
012024

THIS BOOK CONTAINS
RECYCLED MATERIALS

Cover Photo: Leonardo Munoz/VIEW press/Corbis News/Getty Images
Interior Photos: fotostorm/E+/Getty Images, 4–5; Eric Francis/Shutterstock Images, 7, 45; Shutterstock Images, 8, 38 (Reese's), 38 (Kit Kat), 38 (Snickers), 38 (Hershey's), 38 (Skittles); Chris Ison/PA Images/Getty Images, 10–11; Matt Cardy/Getty Images News/Getty Images, 13; Hulton Archive/Getty Images, 15; DEA/Biblioteca Ambrosiana/De Agostini/Getty Images, 18–19; Artur Widak/NurPhoto/Getty Images, 20; Antiqua Print Gallery/Alamy, 23, 43; Peter Summers/Getty Images News/Getty Images, 26–27; Rahman Hassani/SOPA Images/LightRocket/Getty Images, 28; Joe Fox Belfast/Radharc Images/Alamy, 29; Felix Koch/Cincinnati Museum Center/Archive Photos/Getty Images, 31; Roy Rochlin/Getty Images Entertainment/Getty Images, 34–35; Keith Homan/Shutterstock Images, 38 (M&Ms); Africa Studio/Shutterstock Images, 38 (candy corn); Beata Zawrzel/NurPhoto/Getty Image, 39; Andres Kudacki/AP Images, 40

Editor: Laura Stickney
Series Designer: Ryan Gale

Library of Congress Control Number: 2023939654

Publisher's Cataloging-in-Publication Data

Names: Williams, Haley, author.
Title: Halloween / by Haley Williams
Description: Minneapolis, Minnesota: Abdo Publishing, 2024 | Series: History of holidays and festivals | Includes online resources and index.
Identifiers: ISBN 9781098292607 (lib. bdg.) | ISBN 9798384910541 (ebook)
Subjects: LCSH: Holidays--Juvenile literature. | Festivals--Juvenile literature. | Halloween--Juvenile literature. | All Hallows' Eve--Juvenile literature.
Classification: DDC 394.2683--dc23

CONTENTS

A SPOOKY NIGHT

It was the evening of October 31, and Lily was putting on her costume. Dressing up was her favorite part of Halloween. In past years, Lily had dressed up as a vampire, zombie, and skeleton for the holiday. This Halloween, she decided to be a witch.

Lily was excited about her costume. She wore a sparkly black dress and boots with big gold buckles. She also had a tall, pointy witch hat. Lily waited for her friend Blake to arrive so they could go trick-or-treating together.

Popular Halloween costumes include witches, monsters, and movie characters. Some trick-or-treaters use bags or plastic buckets to collect their candy.

PERSPECTIVES

HOLIDAY TRADITIONS

Holidays often involve traditions. Many people practice the same tradition on a certain holiday, such as carving pumpkins on Halloween. Or a family may have a holiday tradition that is unique to them. Michele Brennan is a psychologist. She believes holiday traditions are an important way for people to build bonds. "[Traditions] give us a sense of belonging and a way to express what is important to us," she says. "They connect us to our history and help us celebrate generations of family."

The night before, Blake had come over to Lily's house to carve pumpkins. Blake had carved a scary face into his pumpkin. Lily carved her pumpkin to look like a cat. While they carved pumpkins, the two watched their favorite Halloween movie, *The Nightmare Before Christmas*.

The doorbell rang. Lily grabbed her broomstick, the finishing piece to her witch costume. She ran downstairs to find Blake waiting at the door. He was dressed as a clown. He wore a short rainbow-colored wig, a yellow costume, and a big red ball on the end of his nose.

Jack-o'-lanterns are considered a classic symbol of Halloween. Many people carve faces into their pumpkins, while others carve spooky designs such as bats or moons.

Lily's mom took a picture of them in their costumes. Then the two friends grabbed their candy buckets and ran out into the night. With the full moon out in the sky, Lily knew it was going to be a very spooky Halloween.

WHAT IS HALLOWEEN?

Halloween is one of the world's oldest holidays. It is celebrated every year on October 31. The holiday is often geared toward kids. It is also associated with scary creatures such as ghosts and witches. On Halloween, kids and teens dress up in costumes and go from house to house trick-or-treating. They knock on doors and say

FESTIVALS HONORING THE DEAD

China
Qingming festival
(Tomb Sweeping Day)

Japan
Obon

Italy
Ognissanti
(All Saints' Day)

Mexico
Día de los Muertos
(Day of the Dead)

Ireland
Púca festival

Guatemala
Barriletes Gigantes
(Giant Kites festival)

Many countries around the world have festivals or holidays that honor the dead. Why do you think this might be an important thing for people to celebrate?

"trick or treat" to get candy. Carving jack-o'-lanterns is another common Halloween activity. People hollow out pumpkins and carve designs or faces into them. They put candles inside of jack-o'-lanterns to light them up.

Halloween is celebrated mainly in the United States, Canada, Ireland, and the United Kingdom. Today, it is a secular holiday. But it originated from a religious holiday celebrated in Europe around 2,000 years ago. During that holiday, people believed the spirits of the dead walked among the living. Aspects of this holiday, such as its focus on the dead, can still be seen in Halloween today. Many countries also have holidays that celebrate the dead, such as Día de los Muertos, which is celebrated in Mexico.

Halloween continues to be a popular holiday, especially for kids and teens. It is a time for fun activities and spooky sights. Over the years and with many streams of influence, Halloween evolved into the holiday people observe today.

DÍA DE LOS MUERTOS

Día de los Muertos is celebrated in Mexico and other Latin American countries. It takes place on November 1 and November 2. The name is Spanish for "Day of the Dead." During Día de los Muertos, people honor the dead. Families often create altars to honor relatives who have died. They decorate the altars with items such as food, photographs, and flowers.

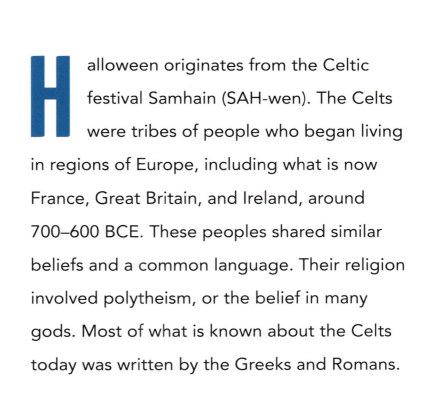

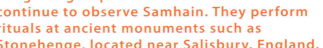

THE ORIGINS OF HALLOWEEN

Halloween originates from the Celtic festival Samhain (SAH-wen). The Celts were tribes of people who began living in regions of Europe, including what is now France, Great Britain, and Ireland, around 700–600 BCE. These peoples shared similar beliefs and a common language. Their religion involved polytheism, or the belief in many gods. Most of what is known about the Celts today was written by the Greeks and Romans.

Religious groups such as Druids and Wiccans continue to observe Samhain. They perform rituals at ancient monuments such as Stonehenge, located near Salisbury, England.

Greek authors first mentioned the Celts between 540 BCE and 424 BCE.

Historians believe the Celts began celebrating the pagan holiday of Samhain around 2,000 years ago. Samhain was the Celtic New Year. It marked the end of the harvest season and the beginning of winter. On the night of October 31, the Celts believed the boundary between the living and dead was at its thinnest. The souls of the dead were said to return from the afterlife. Creatures such as fairies were also said to come out. The Celts believed that people who had died during the year but whose spirits had not yet moved on could cross over into the afterlife during Samhain. These spirits could have one last chance to interact with the living before moving on to the land of the dead.

SAMHAIN CELEBRATIONS

Little is known about the rituals performed during Samhain. However, some scholars believe the celebrations included feasting and drinking to

In Glastonbury, England, people honor their Celtic roots by gathering for the Glastonbury Dragons' Samhain Wild Hunt. This involves performances, intricate costumes, and a parade.

commemorate the end of the harvest. People stocked up on supplies for winter by slaughtering cattle and gathering food from their harvests. Bonfires were also a big part of the holiday. One huge bonfire was lit during Samhain. People from the region traveled to this bonfire and used it to relight the fires in their homes for winter. The bonfire was also used to frighten away evil spirits.

The Celts would disguise themselves to keep evil spirits away as well. People darkened their faces with

PERSPECTIVES

THE HILL OF WARD

The Hill of Ward, also known as Tlachtga, is located in Athboy, Ireland. It is believed to be the location where the Samhain bonfire was lit. People from all over Ireland are believed to have used this bonfire to light the fires in their homes. Steve Davis is an archaeologist. In 2014, he and his team found evidence of burning at the Hill of Ward. The evidence dated back to around 500 CE. Davis said, "We have found evidence of intense burning there, whether you want to equate that with Samhain or not. . . . The medieval texts would associate this very strongly with an annual fire festival."

ash to prevent evil spirits from recognizing them. This was known as guising. Over time, people began wearing masks and costumes to hide their identities instead.

Samhain was also believed to be a good night for fortune-telling. Apples were often used to predict a person's future, predict romances, and search for answers about the unknown. The Celts thought it was easier to foretell a person's future when the boundary between the living and dead was thin.

Apples were traditionally associated with magic and romance. While apple-bobbing was originally seen as a fortune-telling method, it turned into more of a party game.

ROMAN FESTIVALS

In 43 CE, the Roman Empire conquered Celtic lands. Several Roman festivals celebrated or honored the dead, including Parentalia, Feralia, and Lemuria. Parentalia and Feralia were celebrated in February, while Lemuria was celebrated in May. During Parentalia and Feralia, people honored the spirits of their ancestors.

BOBBING FOR APPLES

Bobbing for apples is a fun game that some people play on Halloween. Apples are placed in a tub of water, and players try to grab an apple using only their mouths. The game is connected to the Roman Festival of Pomona. The Romans believed the first person who caught an apple with their teeth would be the first to get married in the new year. They would also peel apples to try to predict the first initial of the person whom they might marry. A person would toss the peel over her shoulder and then see if the peel looked like an initial when it fell on the floor.

Lemuria was a festival dedicated to calming angry or restless spirits. Another Roman festival was the Festival of Pomona. Pomona was the goddess of fruiting trees and orchards.

Eventually, Christianity began to spread across Europe. Christian holidays and festivals began replacing many pagan ones. This included Samhain. However, even though Samhain was being replaced, the holiday and many of its traditions never completely went away.

STRAIGHT TO THE
SOURCE

Many Halloween traditions can be traced back to Samhain. Jack Santino, a former professor of popular culture at Bowling Green State University, discussed these traditions in a lecture:

Halloween is a holiday of many mysterious customs, but each one has a history, or at least a story behind it. The wearing of costumes, for instance, and roaming from door to door demanding treats can be traced to the Celtic period and the first few centuries of the Christian era, when it was thought that the souls of the dead were out and around, along with fairies, witches, and demons. Offerings of food and drink were left out to placate them. As the centuries wore on, people began dressing like these dreadful creatures, performing antics in exchange for food and drink.

Source: Jack Santino. "Halloween: The Fantasy and Folklore of All Hallows." *American Folklife Center*, September 1982, loc.gov. Accessed 3 May 2023.

BACK IT UP

The author of this passage is using evidence to support a point. Write a paragraph describing the point the author is making. Then write down two or three pieces of evidence the author uses to make the point.

THE INFLUENCE OF CHRISTIANITY

Christianity is one of the world's largest religions. During the first century CE, Christianity began to spread across Europe. At first, the Romans did not accept the religion. But in 313 CE, Roman emperor Constantine issued the Edict of Milan. This allowed people to start legally practicing Christianity. About ten years later, Christianity became the official religion of the Roman Empire.

When Pope Boniface IV transformed the Pantheon into a church, he renamed it Santa Maria ad Martyres. It is also known as the church of Santa Maria Rotonda.

Today, some people observe All Saints' Day and All Souls' Day by visiting the graves of their loved ones. They place flowers, candles, and lanterns on the graves.

ALL SAINTS' DAY

The Roman Empire ended in 476 CE, but Christianity continued to spread throughout Great Britain and Ireland. In the early 600s, Pope Boniface IV was head of the Catholic Church. He established All Saints' Day. This holiday, which is still celebrated today, commemorates all Christian saints. All Saints' Day was originally celebrated on May 13, which had also been the final night of the Roman festival Lemuria. On that date in 609 CE, Pope Boniface IV turned the Pantheon, a pagan temple in Rome, into a church. He dedicated it to Christian martyrs and the Virgin Mary, who was the mother of Jesus Christ.

In the mid-700s, Pope Gregory III moved All Saints' Day to November 1. Historians are not exactly sure why Pope Gregory moved the holiday to this date. Some believe this was done to replace the pagan holiday of Samhain with a

TURNIP LANTERNS

Carving pumpkins is a popular Halloween tradition. But people originally carved faces into turnips instead of pumpkins. This idea came from an Irish folktale about a man called Stingy Jack. The story says Jack made a deal with the devil so he would never go to hell. But when he died, Jack was not allowed into heaven either. Jack was forced to roam the world, and he carried a small lantern made of a turnip to light his way. The Irish would hollow out turnips and carve faces in them to protect themselves from evil spirits.

church-related holiday. But some people still continued practicing Samhain traditions. These included lighting bonfires, wearing costumes, and honoring the spirits of the dead.

The name *Halloween* came from All Saints' Day. Another name for All Saints' Day is All Hallows' Day. The word *hallow* means holy. October 31, the day before All Saints' Day, was known as All Hallows' Eve. This was a day for people to prepare for the celebration to honor the saints. All Hallows' Eve later became known as Halloween.

ALL SOULS' DAY

Around 1000 CE, the church established another festival on November 2, the day after All Saints' Day. This festival is known as All Souls' Day. On All Souls' Day, people remember souls who are believed to be in purgatory. In some branches of Christianity, purgatory is a place where the souls of the dead are purified from their sins before going to heaven. All Souls' Day

Instead of prayers, sometimes people going souling would offer to dance, tell a joke, or perform a song in exchange for food. This came to be known as mumming.

became the third and final day of Allhallowtide, the season during which the church remembers the dead.

Some scholars believe All Souls' Day was created as another way for the church to replace pagan celebrations. However, some Samhain traditions were still incorporated into All Souls' Day. People also created new traditions. One important tradition that occurred during All Souls' Day was souling. People in poverty would go door to door offering prayers for the dead in exchange for food called soul cakes. These were

PERSPECTIVES

PAGAN ORIGINS

The pagan origins of Halloween are an important part of its history. Regina Hansen is a lecturer at Boston University. She says that "there are people who won't celebrate Halloween because of its pagan origins and this idea that it's associated with witchcraft." Some religions, such as Christianity and Islam, usually teach that witchcraft is wrong. They often associate witchcraft with evil or the devil. These religions do not support polytheism, either. However, many people who practice these religions still take part in the holiday.

small cakes or biscuits. If people were not given soul cakes, they would threaten to vandalize people's homes. Some scholars believe this tradition may be the origin of trick-or-treating.

Throughout the 1300s and 1400s, people continued to celebrate Halloween as a Christian holiday in connection with All Saints' Day and All Souls' Day. The secular and religious aspects of these holidays had merged. By the 1500s, new religious influences transformed Halloween even more.

STRAIGHT TO THE
SOURCE

Over time, many Christians began associating Halloween with witchcraft and the devil. But today, some groups of people identify as witches or believe in multiple gods. In Lisa Morton's book about Halloween, she discusses these groups and their beliefs:

> *Another group on the fringe of American culture has also claimed Halloween for itself: Wiccans and neo-pagans. In contrast to stereotypical (largely Catholic and medieval) portrayal of the witch as a minion of Satan, modern witches . . . tend to follow a belief system that is benevolent, [centered] in earth worship and free of . . . sacrifice. There are also a wide variety of other neo-pagan beliefs, all of which are polytheistic and which include Shamanism, Druidism and systems based on Norse or Egyptian beliefs.*
>
> Source: Lisa Morton. *Trick or Treat: A History of Halloween.* Reaktion Books, 2019, p. 94.

POINT OF VIEW

After reading this quote, read the primary source from Chapter Two. Each quote presents a different point of view about witchcraft and its association with Halloween. How are they different and why? How are they similar and why? Write a short essay explaining what you find.

COMING TO AMERICA

T he Protestant Reformation was a religious movement that spread across Europe throughout the 1500s CE. Before that time, the Catholic Church was the primary branch of Christianity. But after the Protestant Reformation, several religious groups split from the Catholic Church. They created a new branch of Christianity called Protestantism. The Protestant Reformation had a huge impact on how Halloween was celebrated.

In the United Kingdom, Guy Fawkes Day is also known as Bonfire Night. In some towns, such as Lewes, people celebrate Bonfire Night with costumes and torch-lit parades.

Today, many people continue the tradition of celebrating Guy Fawkes Day with bonfires. Some cities, such as Leeds, put on extravagant bonfire and fireworks displays for the public.

GUY FAWKES DAY

On November 5, 1605, a group of people in England planned to blow up the Houses of Parliament. This is the home of the two branches of the British government. The group was angry at England's King James I because he would not offer more religious tolerance for Catholics. The plan was known as the Gunpowder Plot. During this time, many Catholics were mistreated by Protestants. The goal of the Gunpowder Plot was to kill the Protestant king and reestablish Catholic rule over the throne. However, the plan failed when Guy Fawkes, a member of the group, was caught with explosives. Fawkes and many others from the group were killed or executed. Afterward, the English government made November 5 a national holiday. They called it Guy Fawkes Day.

Guy Fawkes Day became an important celebration for Protestants because it was seen as a victory over Catholics. On the night of the holiday, people celebrated by lighting bonfires, setting off fireworks, and feasting. Children and people in poverty wore masks and went to houses asking for money or treats. When the British came to North America in the early 1600s, they brought many of these traditions with them.

People in Ireland carved faces into turnips and other root vegetables, such as beets and potatoes, to make lanterns. Many of the faces were designed to look scary or angry.

PERSPECTIVES

NO MORE TRICKS

In the early 1900s, American kids would pull a variety of pranks around the time of Halloween. Many adults were angry about these pranks, especially during the years of World War II (1939–1945). During this time, many resources were needed for the war effort. In a 1942 newspaper article, the Superintendent of Schools of Rochester, New York, stated, "Letting the air out of tires isn't fun anymore. . . . It's sabotage. Soaping windows isn't fun this year. Your government needs soaps and greases for the war. . . . Even ringing doorbells has lost its appeal because it may mean disturbing the sleep of a tired war worker who needs his rest."

HALLOWEEN IN THE UNITED STATES

In 1607, the British established their first colony in what is now the United States. It was in Jamestown, Virginia. They continued to start colonies throughout what is now the northeastern United States. One British group that settled in the United States was the Puritans. They were Protestants who believed the church had not distanced

In the early 1900s, many people made homemade Halloween costumes or wore spooky masks. By the 1930s, companies began selling mass-produced costumes.

itself from Catholicism enough. The Puritans had strong religious beliefs. They believed it was wrong to observe holidays that had pagan influences. This included Halloween, All Saints' Day, and All Souls' Day. But the Puritans still celebrated Guy Fawkes Day. The observance of the holiday in the United States continued until the late 1700s.

In the mid-1800s, the Irish began immigrating to the United States due to the Irish Potato Famine. This was a disaster in which a disease destroyed the potato plants in Ireland. Potato crops failed to grow every year between 1845 and 1849. When the Irish came to the

HALLOWEEN CAPITAL OF THE WORLD

The city of Anoka, Minnesota, is known as the Halloween Capital of the World. In 1920, Anoka residents were tired of kids pulling Halloween pranks that damaged their town. Anoka businessman George Green suggested creating a celebration to stop kids from pranking. The town decided to throw a huge parade. Kids dressed up in costumes, and adults handed out treats. Since the first parade, Anoka has continued to celebrate Halloween in this way. Today, people visit the town during Halloween just to witness the festivities.

United States, they introduced Americans to All Hallows' Eve, All Saints' Day, and All Souls' Day. They also introduced the customs of souling and carving turnips, which changed to carving pumpkins.

MISCHIEF NIGHT

In the early 1900s, pranking became a big part of Halloween in the United States. In England, the day before Guy Fawkes Day was called Mischief Night. On this night, children pulled pranks, such as taking neighbors' gates off their hinges.

When Mischief Night was introduced in the United States, American kids caused a lot of trouble. They vandalized homes, businesses, and cars. This continued from the 1920s until the 1950s. In the 1950s, adults began giving kids treats to stop them from pranking. Kids dressed in costumes and went door to door to get their treats. This is when people began using the term *trick or treat*. Throwing Halloween parties to distract kids from pranking also became common. From there, Halloween continued to grow in popularity.

EXPLORE ONLINE

Chapter Four talks about the history of Halloween in the United States. The article at the website below goes into more depth on this topic. Does the article answer any of the questions you had about early Halloween celebrations in the United States?

FOR KIDS: HAUNTED HALLOWEEN HISTORY

abdocorelibrary.com/halloween

HALLOWEEN TODAY

Today, Halloween is one of the most well-known holidays in the United States. It has changed from a religious holiday to a secular one. But many modern Halloween traditions originate from practices dating back to Samhain, All Saints' Day, and All Souls' Day. Today, the holiday is largely geared toward children, but many adults enjoy it as well. Halloween is seen as a time of year when people can wear costumes, watch scary movies, and eat lots of candy.

Many people celebrate Halloween by attending the annual Greenwich Village Halloween Parade in New York City. The event features performers, giant puppets, and creative costumes.

PERSPECTIVES

TRUNK OR TREAT

Trunk or treat is a modern Halloween trend in the United States. It involves people decorating the trunks of their cars. Kids go trick-or-treating between the cars instead of houses. Many parents believe trunk-or-treating is a safer alternative to traditional trick-or-treating. "You know, you're going from trunk to trunk and you're just grabbing the candy and moving on," says Erika Thomas, a parent from Indiana. "Kids are still having fun and they get to wear their costumes and it's safe." Some people say trunk-or-treating provides a safer option because kids can stay in one area instead of going out on the streets during Halloween.

OLD AND NEW

Trick-or-treating and wearing costumes are two of the most popular Halloween traditions. Originally, people dressed up in scary costumes to ward off evil spirits. But today, people dress up in all sorts of costumes. These costumes may be scary, funny, or unique. For example, witches and vampires continue to be classic Halloween costumes. But characters from movies and television shows, such as

Spider-Man or Eleven from the TV show *Stranger Things*, have also become popular costume choices. Carving pumpkins, or jack-o'-lanterns, is another traditional Halloween activity. Instead of carving basic faces in turnips, many people now carve complex designs into their pumpkins.

Food is also an important part of modern Halloween celebrations. Today, the holiday mainly focuses on candy and sweets instead of harvest foods. Candy apples, caramel popcorn, and candy corn are just a few common Halloween treats. Pumpkin-flavored

CANDY CRAZY

In the United States, several holidays are known as candy holidays. These are holidays during which candy sales tend to rise. In the United States, the four major candy holidays are Easter, Valentine's Day, Christmas, and Halloween. Halloween in particular is known as a day for candy because of trick-or-treating. In 2022, Americans spent more than $3 billion on Halloween candy. Chocolate candies are usually the top-selling candy type during Halloween.

FAVORITE CANDIES

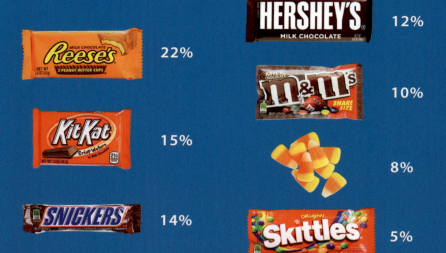

22%

HERSHEY'S 12%

m&m's 10%

Kit Kat 15%

8%

SNICKERS 14%

Skittles 5%

In 2022, a survey asked more than 1,000 adults in the United States about their favorite Halloween candies. What do you notice about the candies on the list? Why do you think more people prefer chocolate candies over other types of candies?

foods and beverages have become very popular as well. The pumpkin spice latte from the coffee company Starbucks is a seasonal favorite across the United States.

Decorations are another big part of Halloween. In 2022, Americans spent around $3.4 billion on Halloween decorations. Many people buy decorations for both the inside and outside of their homes. Some even use these decorations to turn their homes into haunted houses.

Popular Halloween decorations include pumpkins, electric lights, fake skeletons, plastic tombstones, and inflatable figures. Bats, spiders, and zombies are common as well.

HALLOWEEN ON THE BIG SCREEN

For many people, Halloween is a time for scares. Scary movies have become a big part of modern culture. While not everyone enjoys watching them, these movies are seen as a way for people to get into the Halloween spirit. In the United States, interest in watching scary movies continues to rise. From 2014 to 2021, scary movies jumped from 2.7 percent of box office sales to 12.8 percent.

Some movies are considered Halloween classics. One is the film *Halloween*, which was released in 1978.

Some people dress up as characters from Halloween movies, such as Sally and Jack from *The Nightmare Before Christmas*.

It is about a man named Michael Myers who returns to Haddonfield, Illinois, 15 years after killing his sister. As of 2022, *Halloween* is one of the top 100 Halloween movies of all time. There have been many sequels to the film. The thirteenth movie in the series, *Halloween Ends*, was released in 2022.

Other Halloween movies are geared toward kids. *Hocus Pocus* (1993) and *The Nightmare Before Christmas* (1993) are two popular Halloween movies for children. In *Hocus Pocus*, a teenage boy named Max moves to Salem, Massachusetts. He accidently awakens three witches from the 1600s who practice dark magic. The movie *The Nightmare Before Christmas* is about a skeleton named Jack from Halloween Town. After discovering Christmas Town, Jack tries to get Halloween Town to celebrate Christmas instead of Halloween.

Halloween has become a holiday for people of all ages. It continues to be a time for people to come together and take part in old traditions. These traditions have made Halloween into the spooky, candy-filled holiday people celebrate today.

FURTHER EVIDENCE

Chapter Five discusses modern Halloween traditions, many of which originate from early Samhain celebrations. What was the main point of this chapter? What key evidence supports this point? Read the article about the origins of Halloween traditions at the website below. Does the information from the website support the main point of the chapter? Does it present new evidence?

ALL ABOUT THE SPOOKIEST HOLIDAY—HALLOWEEN!

abdocorelibrary.com/halloween

IMPORTANT DATES

Approximately 2,000 years ago
The Celts begin celebrating Samhain on October 31.

43 CE
The Roman Empire conquers Celtic territory.

609
Pope Boniface IV establishes All Saints' Day.

700s
Pope Gregory III moves All Saints' Day to November 1.

Approximately 1,000 years ago
All Souls' Day is established on November 2.

1500s
The Protestant Reformation sweeps across Europe.

1605
The Gunpowder Plot fails in England. Guy Fawkes Day is established on November 5.

1800s
Irish immigrants bring traditions to the United States.

1900s
Pranking becomes a big part of early Halloween traditions. People begin using the term *trick or treat*.

1978
The first movie in the *Halloween* franchise is released.

2022
Americans spend $3.4 billion on Halloween decorations.

STOP AND THINK

Tell the Tale

Chapter Five of this book explores how Halloween is celebrated today. Imagine it is Halloween night. Write 200 words about the celebrations that happen in your community or neighborhood. What traditions do you notice? What sights, sounds, and smells do you experience?

Surprise Me

Chapter Two discusses the origins of Halloween. After reading this book, what two or three facts about the holiday's origins did you find most surprising? Write a few sentences about each fact. Why did you find each fact surprising?

Say What?

Learning about the history of holidays can mean learning a lot of new vocabulary. Find five words in this book you've never heard before. Use a dictionary to find out what they mean. Then write the meanings in your own words and use each word in a new sentence.

You Are There

This book discusses the Celtic holiday Samhain. Imagine you are living in the past and participating in Samhain. Write a journal entry describing your experience. What activities do you do to celebrate? What might you wear to ward off spirits? Be sure to add plenty of detail to your notes.

GLOSSARY

altar
a table or flat-topped block used as the focus for a religious ritual

archaeologist
a scientist who studies ancient peoples and their cultures

boundary
a real or imaginary line that separates two things

commemorate
to honor and give respect to a person or event

folktale
a traditional story typically passed down by word of mouth

immigrate
to move to and resettle in a new country

martyr
a person who is killed because of his or her beliefs

pagan
having religious beliefs that are not part of main recognized religions

secular
not associated with religion

ONLINE RESOURCES

To learn more about Halloween, visit our free resource websites below:

Visit **abdocorelibrary.com** or scan this QR code for free Common Core resources for teachers and students, including vetted activities, multimedia, and booklinks, for deeper subject comprehension.

Visit **abdobooklinks.com** or scan this QR code for free additional online weblinks for further learning. These links are routinely monitored and updated to provide the most current information available.

LEARN MORE

Beer, Julie. *Halloween: 300 Spooky Facts to Scare You Silly*. National Geographic Kids, 2020.

Magrin, Federica. *Atlas of Monsters and Ghosts*. Lonely Planet, 2019.

INDEX

About the Author

Haley Williams is an editor and avid reader who lives in Minnesota. She enjoys watching Halloween movies and decorating for Halloween.